The Pilot Star Elegies

Also by Sherod Santos

The Pilot Star Elegies

SHEROD SANTOS

W · W · Norton

& Company

New York

London

For information about permission to reproduce selections from this book, write to
Permissions, W. W. Norton & Company, Inc., 500 Fifth Avenue, New York, NY 10110.

The text of this book is composed in 11.75/14 Monotype Bembo with the display
set in Poetica Chancery I
Composition by Julia Druskin
Manufacturing by the Maple-Vail Manufacturing Group
Book design by Margaret M. Wagner

Library of Congress Cataloging-in-Publication Data
Santos, Sherod, 1948–
The pilot star elegies / Sherod Santos.
        p.   cm.
    ISBN 0-393-04704-0
    I. Title.
PS3569.A57P55   1999
811'.54—dc21   98-28875
                                                            CIP

W. W. Norton & Company, Inc.
500 Fifth Avenue, New York, N.Y. 10110
http://www.wwnorton.com

W. W. Norton & Company Ltd.
10 Coptic Street, London WC1A 1PU

1 2 3 4 5 6 7 8 9 0

A c k n o w l e d g m e n t s

Grateful acknowledgment is made to the following periodicals, in which some of these poems, or sections of these poems, originally appeared, sometimes in slightly different form:

The Antioch Review, DoubleTake, Field, The Gettysburg Review, The Kenyon Review, The Nation, The Paris Review, Poetry, Quarterly West, Slate, Southern Humanities Review, The Virginia Quarterly Review, Western Humanities Review, and *The Yale Review.* "Abandoned Railway Station," "Belfast Arioso," "The Whelk," "Wing Dike at Low Water," and the opening section of "Elegy for My Sister" (as "Elegy for My Sister") first appeared in *The New Yorker.*

The William James epigraph to "Elegy for My Sister" is from *The Principles of Psychology* (Henry Holt and Co., 1890); the E. M. Cioran epigraph is from *The Temptation to Exist,* translated by Richard Howard (Seaver Books, 1986); the Peter Handke epigraph is from *The Left-Handed Woman,* translated by Ralph Manheim (Farrar, Straus and Giroux, 1977). The epigraph to "The Dream of Exile" is from the *Tristia,* Book III, 8, translated by David R. Slavitt, in *Ovid's Poetry of Exile* (The Johns Hopkins University Press, 1990).

I wish to thank the British Arts Council and the University of Missouri for grants which proved a tremendous help with the writing of this book, and *The Paris Review* for the timely encouragement of the B. F. Connors Prize for "Elegy for My Sister."

I am grateful to a number of people who read and commented on the manuscript for this book, but I'd like to mention three whose suggestions have been especially helpful: Lynne McMahon, David Baker, and Jill Bialosky. Encouragement has come as well in less direct but no less meaningful ways. I wish to thank Deborah Beroset, Elisabeth Marshall, and Lequita Vance-Watkins.

And to those enlightening lifelong fellow travelers—Lynne, Ben, and Zach—I dedicate this book.

Contents

The Pilot Star Elegies

The Story

in memory of M. L. Rosenthal

What are we to make of this story? This is,
after all, the twentieth century, and if any age ever
showed a lack of faith in, among other things,
the structures of a story, surely it must be ours.
It arrived by accident in the afternoon mail,
from a second-hand bookshop in London, a misdirected
copy sent instead of the order I had placed,
months before, for an out-of-print book by a friend.
My friend, who died two weeks ago, was living abroad
at the time, and his lifelong study of the Hebrew elegy
was no doubt mailed to someone waiting, expecting
to receive a copy of the book that I'd received,
Hasidic Tales of the Holocaust. A mistake perhaps
explainable in any number of ways, including
the one my friend had guessed: "Some closet anti-
Semitic clerk who finds such jokes can pass the day."
Nevertheless, in my own stubbornly secular belief
that those very books which we need most
choose us and not the other way around,
I opened the book right then and read,
at the kitchen table, in a small, square panel
of sunlight that framed the closely printed page,
the first of those tales the author recorded
just as she had heard them reported to her.

How late in the middle of a frozen night
in the Janowska road camp, the upper Ukraine,
a voice on the loudspeakers had crackled through,

"You will evacuate the barracks immediately
and report to the field by the vacant lot." In the staggered
confusion that followed, the shouted names
of relatives and friends had filled the air,
and like a broken vessel the barracks soon emptied
in the direction of the field by the vacant lot.
Huddled together against the cold, slowly the prisoners
began to make out, at a distance beyond them
in the looming dark, two wide and freshly dug pits.
Once more, the voice on the loudspeakers crackled through,
"Each of you who values his miserable life
must jump over one of the pits and land on the other side.
For those who fail there is a surprise in store."
And then, as a child imitates machine gun sounds,
ra-ta-tat-tat trailed off into wild, uproarious laughter.

   Among the thousands of Jews in the field that night
was the Rabbi of Bluzhov standing with a friend,
a freethinker from Poland he had met in the camp.
"Rebbe," the friend said, "forgive me, but all our attempts
to jump over the pits are in vain. At best, we'll only
lighten the spirits of the S.S. and those pig-hearted
Ukrainian collaborators. It's just as well that we sit
and wait for the bullets that will end our wretched lives."
"My friend," said the rabbi, turning in the direction
of the open earth, "man must obey the will of God.
If heaven has decreed that pits will be dug
and we will be commanded to jump, then pits will be dug,

and jump we must. And if, God forbid, we fail
and fall into those pits, then we will only reach
the World of Truth a little sooner instead of later."

  The rabbi and his friend were nearing the pits
which were rapidly filling with bodies and,
now that the dark was beginning to lift, looked
a good deal wider than they'd first appeared.
The rabbi glanced down at his feet, the bandaged feet
of a fifty-three-year-old Jew wracked by starvation
and disease. He looked at his friend, a skeleton
with a burning stare. When they reached the edge,
the rabbi closed his eyes and said, "We are jumping!"
And when he opened his eyes, he and his friend
were standing together on the other side. With sudden,
unexpected tears (he thought he'd forgotten *how*
to cry) the friend repeated, "We are here! We are here!
Tell me, Rebbe, how did you do it?" And the rabbi answered,
"I was holding on to the coattails of my father."
And then, staring into the face of his Polish friend,
"But now there is something you must tell me.
How is it that *you* have crossed over to the other side?"
"I was holding on to you," his friend replied.
And neither was sure which was the more miraculous.
And neither was sure that they'd even survived
as anything more than the insane and unvarying wish
of two men leaping headlong into a pit.

When I closed the book, that small, square
panel of sunlight had shifted a little to my left,
so that part of it still leveled across the tabletop,
while the other part lay, halved and unbroken
on the hardwood floor. So far as I could tell,
other than that, nothing much had changed in the world,
perhaps nothing at all had changed in me.
My wife came home a little while later, and, as usual,
we went off to collect our sons from school.
In the following days, I returned the misdirected book,
and the one I'd ordered eventually came.
And that was that: A few years passed, that afternoon
seemed to recede in time, and I didn't really
think about it much anymore. But this morning
after breakfast the week-late posted letter arrived
informing me that my friend had died, and suddenly
it all came back again, as clear to me now
as it was that day, the story of the two men
huddled together at the edge of the pit,
the *ra-ta-tat-tat,* and that small, square panel
of sunlight sliding across the printed page.

One

Of Haloes & Saintly Aspects

Out of a ripple in the sea grass,
two unhoused fiddler crabs
sidestep past the almost-dead

hawksbill turtle turned over
on the beach and left there
staked with a length of broom-

stick and baling wire. The squared,
inquiring head upstraining,
the plastron split, and the sun-

dazed eyes that will not weep
for such incongruities as these:
Faced into the current of an on-

shore breeze, the once-buoyant
cradle of its shell closes like
a trench around its breathing.

Now anchored to the earth,
it founders in the slipstream
of a mild, inverted sea,

and labors toward it still, its little
destiny undisturbed by acts
of forgiveness or contrition.

2. SARAH

Car lights like lanterns in the predawn dark.
The smell of cocoa from a thermos cup.
A light summer shower that comes and goes
against the wipers' fan-shapes ticking closed.

And already my mother, now six years old,
is slipping downward into sleep, a hushed
night music on the radio. She dreams.
And wakes. But what has frightened her?

The sudden vibration of the metal bridge?
The glare? "We're there now, Sarah,"
her father says, as if all of this,
still vaguely seen, has happened before:

the guard politely nodding as they pass;
the space that opens into her each time
they brake to turn onto the tree-lined drive
of the asylum in Staunton, Virginia. Inside,

dressed and attended by a wardroom nurse,
her mother's preparing to meet her guests
(as was her rule) with that look of polite
forbearance she had long ago been widowed to.

3. MINNOWS

The river, while it
runs the gamut of all idle
eyes gathered on the sandbar,
whirlpools in around a snagged
tree-limb trailing the red
flag of the drowned

girl's blouse, though
her body was hauled out
hours ago. Just moments before
that moment, she'd wrestled with
her brothers while her father
spilled a dipnet full

of minnows in a
Mason jar, and now the jar,
the net, the flattened reeds beside
their fishing poles, remain as they
could not help but remain;
now, with a swift

almost unconscious
purpose such daily rituals
compose in time, the coptered-in
reporter from the *Post Dispatch*
opens up her notebook
and tries again

to get it down in
just that way: the sloped
sand shelf at the river's bend;
the trailing blouse; those min-
nows still blindly bump-
ing at the glass.

4. JEFFERS COUNTRY

The town the wealthy come to, not overly
concerned with how the clerks and waiters
here drive cars expensive as their own—
a *fin de siècle* Marxist dream it's great to kill

a weekend in. Bay leaves season the air
along Ocean Avenue, which dips down
to the beach, that cypress-lined, granite-faced
allegory he worried into something more

inhuman than a paradise of sticks and stones.
A doubled bell-tone echoes off the Carmelite
mission's stuccoed walls, and now
the bride and bridegroom, pausing a moment

in the portico, will feel their backlit shadows
dwell in the house of a Lord grown congenial.
He imagined the strophe and antistrophe,
the steelhead nosing at the riverbank,

the banked warheads nosing underground,
but here the Empire's less like Shiva
than the motel's picture postcard,
where a gelid harvest moon looms above

Point Lobos, as though a great dog,
startled from sleep, had opened its eye.
And, he wondered, we wonder why
treetops and people are so shaken.

5. DALAI LAMA

From between the pages
of a nineteen sixty-eight junk store
copy of D'Aulaire's *Norse Gods and Giants*:
the five clean-cut crenelate petals
of a flower almost alchemical
   in its papery

  likeness to what
it was: a sign conspired
to preserve some tremor in an adolescent's
heart, to round out phyla in a science
notebook kept for school,
   or perhaps, in fear,

  to summon the wandering
Valkyries whose muraled lives
are marked for good by the cinnabar
leached off its cells. Now, a dead
metaphor carrying on long
   past its paradigm

  of human need,
it faces into the future
freed of our small demands on it,
like the exiled Tibetan god-king
blessed with the common sense
   to survive himself.

6. THE RESTORATION

The one-armed pencil seller at the Place des Vosges
spins out drum rolls on a tin can topped
with aluminum foil, so dexterously—

three pencils, one between each finger of his remaining hand—
passersby are momentarily distracted from
the unsheathed stump,

which gestures (and would soon repel, its raw, rubbed weight
like a face whose features have smudged away),
gestures, nods, conspires

to reign the twice-blind sovereign of a cardboard box
no one dares look into . . . scattering coins
like flower petals at the Sun King's feet.

7. RIMBAUD

I

My dog-collared spirit delirium's damned
(the Belgian jailer swears to me) to haul out
slop buckets for centimes. Yet still I perfume
with rosewater—dope's scented shadow-king!—

my female airs, my crippled coupling rhymes.
Scatologiste is my nom de plume, *Poète*
my nom de guerre . . . Don't think I care. I've dragged
the corridors of High Art and I'm bored as God.

I I

But who *is* God? And what Aeschylean
star-chart, what alchemy of sins, foresaw
the day that I'd become the voice
of His abandoned room? And at what cost?

It scares me still when I am high and He reels
suddenly through the dark, like the red-haired
teenage gasoline girl who one night crashed
the barricades with her clothes awash in flame.

I I I

When I wake, it is noon. I find myself
spread out like a banquet on the barracks floor,
a boy whose body is inhabited,
a sea-garden where great sperm whales spawn.

I now view childhood differently, as through
a lens that memory's vaselined: tears,
threats, an operatic gloom—love's ceremonies!—
and mother's tirades like the fleur-de-lis.

I V

Memento mori: old dreamboat, poor Paris,
a hundred years from now your well-heeled, fame-
gored poets will invoke my royaled name,
make my self-loathing seem an empery. Look,

I've made nine angels weep, I've toed the line,
I've been a bad mother to my infant soul.
And yet, like poetry's Dog Star I'll still rise,
a great drunken fly in the toilet bowl!

V

I gouged out Reason's eyes. And now I see
the gelded Bridegroom my fond Vision's wed:

two faces disfigured on the marriage bed
while want winds round them like a barber's pole.

Forgive me? Don't kid yourself. I'll get mine
when that death's-head called Posterity scrawls
my epitaph: a foul-mouthed, queening malcontent
hunting the hound-spirit of some future god.

8. PORTRAIT OF A COUPLE AT CENTURY'S END

Impatient for home,
the after-work traffic fanning out along
the wet streets, a jagged sound,
like huge sheets of construction paper torn
their length, and through

the walls, the shudder
of the furnace, as though a hundred thousand
bottle-flies were trapped between
the clapboards and the plaster. A gentler
rain blows across

the TV screen, where
a CNN foreign correspondent tells
how a single Serb mortar shell
just leveled the crowded terrace of a
Tuzla café.

The darker crimes are
faceless in that lidless, immemorial
eye *(a world outside, a world
within)*, so summer's what they talk about,
the meal, their work,

and how they quarrelled
one night in Iowa. The buried longings

such memories stir. And yet,
in what they can't express they remind us
of something too,

of something we've felt
settle on our lives, in shadow-life of ours.
So forget for a moment
the future of their monogamous hearts,
forget the rain,

the traffic, the boot-
soles pressed forever in our century's mud,
for it's all there, whatever
they'd say, the industry of pain, the Ho-
ly Spirit of

everything that's been
taken away, it's all there in the burnt match-
head preserved into amber
by a beeswax candle pooling beside
their dinnerware.

Pilot Stars

Open window; eucalyptus scent; the ever-slightly
slackening heat. Given the way the day has gone,
she's waited awhile to turn off the lamp in the guest room
which, she remembers, had once been the room
her mother kept when the two of them were fighting.
She has come home to visit her father, an Air Force pilot
retired for years, who lives alone, and who, he'd
written her late last week, was "discovered with a form
of cancer." Her father hasn't wanted to speak of it;
she has tried to press him. Like most people
of her generation, unlike those of his, she believes
such talks are compulsory, some tested proof
of a power in words all evening she'd kept insisting on,
to the point that they have argued in ways (and,
most likely, from similar needs) they had throughout
what he still calls her "college days." Three hours later,
and she can't help feeling . . . what?—angry,
frightened, ashamed of herself for upsetting him
when she'd really only wanted to comfort.
It just doesn't have to be like this. And yet of course
she knows it does. Knows what's set in motion now
will be there at the end. And so, lying in bed
with the lamp still on, she closes her eyes and tries to sleep,
closes her eyes and watches the way the blood
wells up behind the lids and, mixed with tiny specks
of light, becomes a night sky flecked with stars.
And it's as if through the dark of memory they've come,
all sensed and intended and pointing a way
when the frozen compass locks in place

in the green-glow cockpit's chill, where it's 1956
and she's sailing above the ocean ten thousand feet
in her father's lap, sustained by an ancient
spine-ticking shine and watching his free hand
check them off on a night map figured with a sextant:
Lyra, Cygnus, Aquila, resetting the crosshairs,
then banking west toward a hunter's moon,
and like another constellation purled out on the dark,
the islands slowly rolling over the far-flung
boundaries of the southern sky. And it's on her skin
as she's lying there, the salt and shine
of leaning into him through the tight half-circle
of that moonward bend, then leveling it out,
leveling the world in one loosening turn
for a girl lightheaded at the prospect of a life
taken up somehow on the scattered narratives
of all those names, those heart-logged syllables
by which her father had found a way
(o, how far the fall from childhood seems)
to chart his passage between heaven and earth.
From the quiet in the house, her father might've been
asleep by then. It was after one. The heavy air
of late September still hung stock-still in the lamplit room.
Then as had happened for the last two nights—
had she not stayed awake to listen? would she not
stay awake for nights to come?—the footsteps began,
back and forth in the upstairs room, the slow,
incessant, solitary dying that would go on
another eighteen months, and by which it seemed

some terrible mourning had already begun
to extinguish the light-points one by one,
until the dark like the dark she fell through then
was suddenly storyless, boundless, and blank.

T w o

Spring Elegy

for Frank Vincent, my student,
who died of AIDS, 3.17.97

All morning in class that hollow feeling of how little
we've been left to say; and then, a few hours later,
while I was downstairs checking the afternoon mail,
someone came in and laid out neatly on my office desk
a black-and-white photograph, a sprig of forsythia,
and a tenth share of his ashes in a smoked glass vial.

The Book of Hours

Late August, and once again the frail moon's launched
like an air balloon off the flat-roofed campus bookstore.
Once again, the night watch takes his cake and coffee
on the concrete bench just below my window.
The twelve taped chimes of the clock tower bell,
the twelve short echoes that follow. A silence, then,
through the indrawn *shush* of the library doors,
two exhausted students, stunned to reenter
the womb-weight of the humid air, linger
for a moment to say goodbye before lugging
their heavy backpacks off in opposite directions.
How many years will this scene go on repeating itself?
How many years before one of them takes
the other's hand, and the poem is brought to an end?

Borage

We're cleaning up after the guests have gone,
the two of us drying the last of the dishes,
a little lightheaded from all of the wine,
a little too familiar with that touch of melancholy
that lingers in the air after parties these days.
Then somehow or other it comes around
I ask about him, who he was, and how was it,
anyway, it happened. But there's not that much
she remembers, truly, there is scarcely anything
at all. Oh, his eyes, perhaps . . . and then,
now that she thinks of it, wasn't it his first time
as well? . . . Yes, his eyes, she remembers, his eyes
when he entered her, his eyes were the same
uncomplicated blue of borage or deep water.

The River-God of Rocheport

Like an old idea that's lost for years then taken up again
against new claims, the waters swelled their failing banks
to flood this little river town, whose fuel-oil tanks,
abandoned cars, raw-wood houses and gardens
sank back beneath that shallowed world one road led out of
hopefully, as if out of that great abundance from which
all things come to make their lives escaping from,
relinquished to, a fate grown darker in the light of day.

And there, at the roadside, standing outside their pickups
as the sky cleared to a watery blue, the townspeople
gathered on the new shore of their past lives that,
like prescient dreams, reflected them in their absence.
It was as though, not a river but a river-god had appeared
to them, its glittering image poured out along
the limestone bluffs in a likeness they now came to see
was more familiar than they'd ever imagined

a god might be, as though somehow out of what they felt
had spilled this heavily welling ache, the vast
reverberation of claims their families once had staked
in this low-lying midwestern valley. And they conceived of it
as possible that all around them, everywhere, everything
fattened on light and rain, every herb, cornstalk, cricket, grub,
every heron call and fossil stone, was somehow linked
to what that was they now must summon to rebuild their lives.

And so it happened that one by one as evening fell
that night in June, the pickup trucks backed up the hill,

a few stayed on, and their partings for all they left behind,
for all the poverty of their goodbyes, proved a meaning
they'd cling to in the days ahead, until the glad time came,
as it has come, to signal from storefronts, fence posts,
and jambs how in the summer of nineteen ninety-three
a river called Missouri had risen this high.

The Whelk

for Ralph Santos

Remember? Turned up by our half-blind
sheltie in the backyard garden one afternoon
after we'd just moved in: a chipped,
hand-sized lightning whelk carried at least

two thousand miles to outlast that chunk
of recently developed farmland where,
aeons ago, fishes swam through a coral sea.
And yet vague as such things were to us,

we somehow dated its arrival to the first
prairie schooner days, and imagined it was
smuggled that far enearthed in a trunk
with the flannel night-clothes and underthings,

and treasured no doubt for its ridged,
opalescent slant across the salt-scoured surface
of its nacreous skin. But then in the face
of god knows what geologic calamity,

it's lost one day, thrown out in the rush
of a highway robber's search for rings,
or buried perhaps in a simple wake
for its hopelessly stranded, landlocked owner,

who was, or so I've come to think,
like "Helen of Colorado Springs,"
inclined to tears each August when
poppies ran like torchmen with the wheat.

And all of that only to find its way
above the sink on our kitchen window,
a familiar from another's life
resettled for a summer into ours,

where I can see it still, like a face back-
lighted at the front porch forty years ago,
its breathless *allie in come free*
calling us home from the evening.

Fermanagh Cave

An emerald dungeon's blacklight glow
glimmered in the deeper reaches
where my son and I could hear the slub
of water riddling through the muck.

We'd stumbled on it following a stream,
his first cave made stranger still
by a chill that closes on the goblined heart
of a boy inflamed by stories where

gnome-clans hoarded underground
bone-shard, mandrake, monkey gland,
and eel. And so, grave Hansel
paying out his last scraps of bread,

he inched inward looking back
and gathering himself as he devolved
step by step along the wet-ribbed walls,
the omphalos seepage of a subterranea

that dreamed us into its kingdom come,
where like some secret dreams
make known the burnt-punk smell
of marijuana cluttered up the air,

and just beyond, just close enough to see,
a spur of light that like a dwindling
eyemote disappeared. Then the sound
a human soul makes as it slips out

from the throat. Composed in darkness,
my son's hand closed on mine. I bent
to whisper we could turn back now,
but his voice was there before me saying,

"Something's here." And something was,
something that in that instant rose,
and moved off from us, or drew up close.
In either case, my son came to me

almost weightlessly at first, then hungry
for what was filling up my arms,
the startled, upriding bodyweight
of a boy I'd never before felt rock

so solidly into the place I was,
blind and hunkered in the earthen air.
I held him only a moment there.
We didn't speak. And though the wheeze

of his breathing must've stopped my ears,
for weeks to come, settling him back
to sleep at night, or waking him
from some troubling dream, I'd hear

the soft concussion of an outsized heart-
beat I could not decide was mine,
or his, or the stranger's I had brought us to.
Or if what happened would happen again,

years from now, when he is grown,
and I have grown newly strange to him.

Tahoe Nocturne

Do you have the poems of Han-shan in your house?
Han-shan asks at the end of his poem. Cold mountain.
Ice-flowers on the windowpane. Exhausted from sledding
all afternoon, the boys have dragged their sleeping bags out
in front of the fire, Lynne under blankets beside them.
Having earlier drawn the shortest length of broomstraw,
I've been sitting up reading by lantern light
these words that no one will believe. Now, past midnight,
rising to bank up hardwood for that slow burn through
till morning, and I suddenly recall my childhood wish
to live invisibly, to close my eyes and not be seen.
A fear of death? I think perhaps the opposite: a desire
to escape the life of facts. A thousand, ten thousand miles . . .
Do you recognize me, air, where once I wandered?

Three

ELEGY FOR MY SISTER

We ought to say a feeling of and, a feeling of if, a feeling of but, a feeling of by, quite as readily as we say a feeling of blue or a feeling of cold. Yet we do not: so inveterate has our habit become of recognizing the existence of the substantive parts alone, that language almost refuses to lend itself to any other use.

   —WILLIAM JAMES, *The Principles of Psychology*

A vague, faintly outlined idea. . . . Then from the furthest reaches of the self, in sonorous transfiguration, may be heard a noise, a sound, a tonality which by its very insistence must either paralyze us forever or preserve our life anew.

   —E. M. CIORAN, *The Temptation to Exist*

In the daylight she sat in the rocking chair on the terrace. The moving crowns of the pine trees were reflected on the window behind her. She began to rock; she raised her arms. She was lightly dressed, with no blanket on her knees.

   —PETER HANDKE, *The Left-Handed Woman*

Elegy for My Sister

Sketchbooks. Night fires. Aesop and Grimm.
An electric model of the Lipizzaner stallions
circling each other in her darkened room.
An empty schoolyard after a morning rain,
and a figure eight traced by bicycle tires,
over and over, without a flaw. Her vine-
borne flowering marginalia (flowering now

in the ever-widening margins of memory).
The up-early privacy of a house at dawn;
a jigsaw puzzle, disarranged, arranging
into evergreen leaves on a holly tree (the
quick bird-movements of her slender hands).
The window she'd look in each time
we'd pass the Home for Retarded Children.

A doll whose name changed day by day,
and an imaginary friend she called "Applause."
My feeling (no doubt hopelessly tinged
with how, were she here, her looks alone
would resist my attempts to say these things)
that all of this was already lost, even then.
The Palace of Nowhere. L'Hôtel de Dream.

1.

It comes back to me just this afternoon—
could it really be thirty-five years ago?—
as though, through the scumbled leafage
of that wooded past, some sunlit clearing
had opened out for one bright moment
then vanished back into the gathering dark:
It was late in the day, as I recall,
her pinking winter-white shoulders bent
over the backyard flower beds, soggy still
from the snowmelt that week
loaded underground, at body heat, in April.
Bolstered by pillows, I'd stayed inside,
my headcold clearing in the camphored room,
though I wasn't simply imagining things
when I watched a field rat bore back out
from the mulch pile tumbled behind her;
or when, sinking her pitchfork into the banked
hay bales, a blacksnake speared by the tines
wound up like a caduceus along the handle.
Nevertheless, there she is, made over again
by my own deliberate confusions: bare-
shouldered, burning, imperiled in the yard.

2.

. . . . And so it is I begin
this now, a week after my sister's suicide,
for I can already feel her slipping beyond
the reach of words, and words like bread crumbs
trailed behind her on the forest floor
are her way back to us, or us to her,
through the seasonless weathers of the afterworld.
But I begin this for another reason as well,
a more urgent and perhaps more selfish reason,
to answer that question which day by day
I fear I'm growing less able to answer:
Who was she whose death now made her
a stranger to me? As though the problem
were not that she had died, and how was I
to mourn her, but that some stalled memory
now kept her from existing, and that she
could only begin to exist, to take her place
in the future, when all of our presuppositions
about her, all of those things that identified
the woman we'd buried, were finally swept aside.
As though the time of her being remained,
as yet, a distant premonition within us.

3.

Well, that's what life's like. She'd say this
whenever she couldn't imagine what else
to say, or how her mind might disengage
that darkening shape-shift she could feel
was somehow, through her, handed down,
mother-to-daughter, daughter-to-child,
like the watercolors in her light-green eyes.
At the graveside, her two unkneeling daughters
closed in mute parenthesis around that space
(Sarah Ballenger Santos Knoeppel),
as if the soul encircled might re-create the ground
of being she'd unnamed—or lend new hope
to that vague impossibility: *Someone to love her*
for who she was . . . A love I fear even she
finally felt incapable of when tears surprised
her stonewalled heart with what she'd done.

4.

Her hair was dark and irregularly parted,
and there was something undecided in the way
she chose to present herself to the world,
though her power over others (if not herself)
seemed to come from the confidence
of someone who felt she'd suffered more,
and so, perhaps rightly, assumed she possessed
the kind of spirit most favored by God.
But there was always something in the way
she dressed—an oversized brooch, a man's
sports watch, a garish hat or neck scarf—
which attempted to reverse that odd impression,
like those cowering dogs that so often appear
in seventeenth-century religious paintings.
Those mongrel shapes that seem added to counter
some otherwise unabated spiritual yearning.

5. *(State Hospital, Nashville, Tennessee, 1979)*

Behind the fretted network of a wrought-
iron grille, she stood untouched by the holiday
lights strung haphazard in Admissions,
a ticked synaptic flicker, first in amethyst,
then in flame. Convalescent, bloodshot,
unreachable, she watched the freaky light
motes flare against the doubled panes
seventeen years ago, and now, beside
her tray of stubbed-out cigarette ends,
she takes out a hand mirror and looks again
past that figure drawn up suddenly, as through
a wide theoptic eye, at that something
going on inside in ways the shocked brain's
weird illogic strains to accelerate and shelter.

6.

She was born *Sarah Gossett Ballenger*—
Sarah our mother's proper name, *Gossett* our mother's
family name, *Ballenger* the name of her father.
Following our mother's second marriage,
her name was changed to *Sarah Ballenger Santos,*
and when she herself got married, she became
Sarah Ballenger Santos Knoeppel. After her divorce, she changed
her name to *Sarah Beth Ballenger,* though *Beth*
was selected simply because she "liked its sound,"
and because, for once, she'd felt entitled to name herself.

Following a stillbirth in the twelfth year
of her marriage, she instructed her daughters
to refer to her as *Mimi*—not *Mommy,* not *Mother,*
not *Mom.* At some point after she'd left home
(she was sixteen or seventeen at the time),
she changed the spelling of her familiar name
from *Sally* to *Salley,* and of her proper name
from *Sarah* to *Sara,* though here too the reasons
she gave were largely a matter of preference:
she just found those spellings more "personal."

Thus all her life she felt her name referred to a presence
outside herself, a presence which sought to enclose
that self which separated *her* from who *they* were.
Thus all her life she was never quite sure who it was
people summoned whenever they called her by her name.

And, more specifically, she was never quite sure
they recognized *her* when, and if, she responded.
As she put it, at various periods in her life
she'd "lent" herself to particular names, only to reclaim
herself in time, only to "suppose" all over again.

7.

My sister left no note behind. This was reason enough for some in the family to believe her death an accident, not a willful act, not a suicide. In the days before the funeral, my mother was given to saying to those who called on the phone, "She just died, that's all." But saying it with a tone of besieged impatience, so as to cut off further questioning.

Her appearance in the casket had a symbolic meaning perhaps lost to anyone outside the family. The clothes my mother had chosen for her recalled that time, twenty years earlier, when she'd struggled for months to impersonate the life of an "ordinary" person. A black knit sweater with roses embroidered across the chest. A full frill collar. A "virginity pin." A knee-length, wine-colored, lambs-wool skirt.

Her hands were folded *peacefully* on her chest; her nails were done up *tastefully*; her head was cushioned on a silken pillow in an attitude of *calm repose*. Preparations meant, not to recall her "as she was in life," but to bestow on her the equanimity (or perhaps, more truly, the respectability) her life in our eyes had always lacked.

One of my sister's daughters brought a small white dog to both the viewing and the funeral. Her explanation: "He's like one of the family." And, as it happened, the dog was both *silent* and *respectful* throughout the protracted ceremonies.

During the funeral there was a very old woman who stood "on guard" directly behind the casket. She wore enormous sunglasses with wide black stems (like the glasses of the blind) and supported a cross that was mounted on a staff—the kind that choristers carry in church. My mother later told me that she was there in order to assist the minister. But what did she assist him in doing? And what did she represent?

I wasn't at all bothered by the occasional laughter at the viewing, nor by the heavy, perfumey air from the flowers, nor by the looming presence of the funeral directors. In fact, I found them strangely consoling, as if they'd signaled some sort of clear-cut wrong, some unequivocal breach of faith, in a sea of otherwise ambiguous and ambivalent gestures of mourning. It wasn't until the viewing was over, and my mother asked that a blanket be laid over her daughter's body, that I even felt the urge to cry. And even then it wasn't until my mother remembered how cold it had been—"bone-chillingly cold"—at the burial of her mother.

8.

Forgiving, unforgiving, fierce, the way memory's
shadings return us to such sure and simple
self-revealing truths: her life, her death,
her decision to take them both in hand
and like twin daughters summoned home
lead them back from the future. Yet sometimes
I see my sister still, see her as though
from the back of my mind, in the black-and-white
of an earlier time, a time before words
colored in to phrase those meanings fleshed out
from the trembling backdrop of their shadow play.

And in black-and-white I see her now, striped
by streetlight through the window blinds,
ghosting our recently moved-in house which,
ghosted by those who'd just moved out,
seemed cast in the cramped otherworldly dark
of a photo negative some caustic's spent.
Rolled from bed, I'd stumbled to find a noise
in the kitchen, the tap turned on, and a muffled sobbing
like a sorrow in the walls, like something
that's rooted in the house's heart. A flanneled
shade convulsed by tears, she shouldered past me

into the back bedroom where my mother and father
were waiting for her—in darkness or light,
I can't recall. From where I stood, I thought

she might've been lost in sleep, her grief so like
a belief in something stripped of particulars,
outside words, or outside what I imagined words,
strung like beads along the thread of some un-
settling dream, were suddenly powerless
to articulate. For over and over my mother pleaded,
"Say it, Sally. Say it, please. Just call him—
father—once for us. Say it so we both can hear."

And my sister weeping, "I can't, I can't,"
as though nothing in the world could make her,
no punishment, outrage, exile, fear, renounce
the vision she'd received that day. But the world,
as it now seemed to me, would reverse itself
in time to see the bright up-gathering miracle of it
fluoresce our house like a candle's flame.
For the pleadings had ended, the sobbing too,
and strangely enough (could this be true?)
I lay down outside their door and slept
the deep sleep of the Blessed-by-Sorrows.

9.

As a rule, my sister didn't care for social gatherings,
though when she went she carried away
a palpable feeling of euphoria. This wasn't,
however, the euphoria of "a good time,"
but the accomplishment of someone who'd managed
to remain *incognito* under very exacting scrutiny.
When we were alone, this shyness proved self-
wounding, and I felt at times that many of the secrets
she confessed to me were things she actually
wished she regretted, more than things she suffered
for having done. In these and other respects,
she reminded me of those blue translucent birds
("so the hawks can't see them against the sky")
Marlon Brando describes in *The Fugitive Kind.*
Those legless birds that "don't belong no place
at all," and so stay on the wing until they die.

10.

She woke near six and once again she found
the bed behind the draw curtains turned out bare,
a blue-beating line of light mounting
like a migraine on the plasticine.
On the television screen, the patriot-assassin
climbed from the wreckage of his bombed-out car,
the very same car the ads now claimed
would "take you where you'd never dream."
A small pot of pink impatiens, and the belled
fire of evening as it drained off slowly
from the windowsill (her lamplit, high strung
folding bed like a river-rounded island city
against which the darkness lapped and rose).
And then the full bodyweight of it: the pin-
prick of consciousness breaking on the skin,
and the suddenly unroofed outreach in.

11.

Because of her "instability," doctors were reluctant
to write her prescriptions, though she was very adept
at describing those symptoms which called for the drugs
she wanted. She was also doggedly persistent.
One physician I telephoned defended his decision
by relating how, during one of her many unscheduled visits,
she'd remained in his office refusing to leave
until he'd written her a script for sleeping pills.
To be "cautious," he had written it out for only half
the normal number of pills. Which perhaps explains why,
on the floor beside her bed they found the empty vials
for four different drugs, each one ordered by
a different doctor—meprobamate, propoxyphene,
amitriptyline, and carisoprodol—a lethal combination
of antianxiety agents, painkillers, antidepressants,
and muscle relaxants. Clearly, killing herself
required the same cunning, and the same unspoken
complicity of others, that she'd needed to stay alive.

12.

Several days after the funeral, while watching
a home movie of my niece's wedding, I feel suddenly
and hopelessly incriminated—like the criminal
in some detective story who discovers his victim's
ghost in the crowd—when the camera pans past
my sister seated in one of the folding chairs.
But what guilt, or sadness, was I hiding from?
The knowledge that nothing I'd done had helped?
The fear that I'd done nothing at all? That brief
but nonetheless clear sensation, when the phone call came,
that it was finally over with, finished, and done?
This evening, while I was downstairs working
at the kitchen table, I could hear my wife scolding our son
for marking with crayons on the bedroom wall.
"Aren't you ashamed of yourself?" she asked him.
And I couldn't help thinking, "Yes, I am."

13.

Visiting her in the hospital, I became increasingly aware
of a narrowing silence in the way she spoke,
a silence in her gestures, a silence in her face and eyes,
a silence between, but also *through,* her words,
as if her being were somehow carried along
on the soundless current that composed her mind.
This added to her already enormous fund of anonymity,
and gave her speech, not an air of distraction,
but the unexpected sharpness of someone who,
having something to say, says nothing at all.
It wasn't until the long drive back in the evenings
that I'd realize how fully I'd entered that silence,
how immersed I'd been in the *she* she was,
and it required a concerted effort on my part—
turning up the radio, talking out loud—
before I could go back to feeling like myself again.

14.

The last time I saw my sister was two days after Christmas.
As my taxi to the airport pulled away from the curb,
she stood at the front door of her apartment house
and watched me go. In memory (which is to say,
in the theater of regret and hopefulness) there is a lightness
about her that is hard to explain by description
or imagination, as if, already, some part of her being
had relinquished its watery hold on her—
as if, like a woman standing under a falling star,
she'd momentarily assumed the stance of someone
whose fate is now certain. Nevertheless, I think:
this is an image that has survived her, a likeness freed
from the raveling constraints of what no longer is. I think:
This is an image she wouldn't have struggled against.

15.

A print of Audubon's ovenbirds hung above
our parents' king-sized bed: the female,
ornamental in her tawny crown, cranes
along a branch the male has vectored off of
like a fighter plane; and below them both,
the nest whose domed, combustible form
has given them their name, and whose heat,
my sister explained to me, kindled the air
around married lives. Sometimes early
on the winter weekends, we'd crawl into bed
with the two of them, sink down under
that gossamer of warmth, that place of being,
and dream ourselves awake again, and waking
wonder what it was could make that space ignite,
inflame them so.   One night, or so my sister's
story goes, from across the hall she'd watched them
after they'd just come back from a dinner party,
or an evening out. Mother was lying fully clothed,
face down on the coverlet, my father was standing
beside her with his hands raised up above his head,
a wildness in the way he pitched there blindly
and would not move. At first I'd imagined this
must be grief, a rehearsal for mourning, a game
we too had sometimes played: my sister's slow,
theatrical death (she'd drop like Brier Rose
to the palace floor), my own inconsolable loss

dispersed in angers beside her shade,
*Don't leave me, don't leave me, don't leave
me alone.*
        The next part was less clear to me.
Having risen suddenly from the dead, how Mother
reached up to draw my father down to her, draw him
into her warming arms, where she (inexplicably)
stroked his hair. *So what happened next?* I had to ask,
for this story seemed to have no point or end.
"Well, it was like they both decided to scream."
But did they really? Did they scream? And why,
I asked her, why do they call that "making love"?
But already she's drawing the shoebox out
from beneath the bed, dividing old buttons into two
small piles and shuffling the deck for a game of Eights.
For over an hour we do not speak, though the game
will drag on endlessly, my left hand burying
the face cards, my sister's laughter bracketing
the air every time one of hers gets played.

16.

We waited at the back gate where the other
patients were less likely to wander big-eyed
past the orderlies, and in the check station's
neutral stump of shade, about to say goodbye,
she came down suddenly from her high room,
focused, then let go a web of Seconal
from her frazzled hair, as though in one whoosh
from a blowgun out beyond the cyclone fence,
a tipped dart grazed her temple quick
to restore her wounded stare. "Sometimes I feel
like a balloon blown up well beyond its limits . . ."
A figure of speech she stepped back from
and appeared to ponder as if from afar, as if,
at last, she had described herself to herself.

17.

After she left the hospital she decided to try
and make a new start. That's why she moved to Dallas.
The heat. The activity. The unending sprawl.
Everything stood for something else. It was also the time
she suddenly began to look on popular stereotypes—
"the suburban housewife," "the responsible neighbor,"
"the loving parent"—as complex paradigms
for how to live, as if every gesture of conformity
had the power to suggest how out of sync
her life had been, how far removed from a world
where problems solved themselves simply by virtue
of who you are. This was, perhaps, one reason why
the television came to seem to her both promising
and reproachful, an array of vaguely idealized forms
whose norms of behavior had always remained
just beyond her reach. Which is why, when she watched it,
she appeared to watch it *religiously*, the way
a medieval mind might've given itself to a gathering
of saints and angels. It's a time her children
would refer to later as the only truly happy moment
in her life. But since, by then, they measured her life
by degrees of despair and unhappiness, it remained
for them the least tellable part of her story. That year,
from nineteen eighty-three to nineteen eighty-four,
was eventually reduced to a bloodless abstraction:
THE HAPPIEST PERIOD IN HER LIFE

18.

My sister's habit in the last few years of referring
to her periods of depression, black, prolonged
periods she was helpless to either prevent or end,
as "another bout of the flu." In that way, she could see
what happened inside of her not as the fitful clash
of antagonistic forces, but as the mind's own
seasonal movement in time, where things
all seemed to come and go (as the poets say)
"as naturally as the leaves to the tree." In truth,
these intervals led to disabling spells of "unreality"—
not ill-being, not well-being, but non-being.
The electroshock treatments fifteen years before
were the closest analogy she could think of:
"That instant just after, when the convulsions stop,
and you're not sure where, or even who, you are."

19.

"Face it!" This said with such urgency,
her daughters can't tell if it's herself she's talking to,
or him. "I just can't live like this anymore."
It's over, finished, the gesture forged as finally
as the front door slamming, or their memory of it,
and makes the glass panes of the china cupboard . . . shine?
Because the sun's just struck the oriel casement?
Because the house is exonerated one last time?
It hurt to see her daughters see what they couldn't,
in their hearts, quite pity. And yet, across
a lesser distance they'll recall a stunted,
uninclining sadness when, six months later,
they return from a weekend trip to find
two note cards thumbtacked to the doorframe:
"I keep coming back but no one's home."
And: "You mustn't forget I'm still your mother."

2 0 .

She was someone about whom people remarked:
She never seemed to find a life for herself. Or:
Her life was the story of a long collapse, its end
a dark, unlucky star she'd clung to hopefully,
for better or worse. Shortly after her death,
we discovered in her closet a large box containing
countless bottles of lotions, powders, lipsticks,
and oils. Many of them had never been opened,
still others had barely been used at all.
Sorting through the contents it occurred to me
the box contained some version of herself,
some representation of who she was—
a stronger, more serene, more independent self?—
that she'd never had the chance to become.
Sorting through the contents it occurred to me:
She once was becoming; she now ceased to become.

21.

Is it inconceivable (I suspect this question haunts
us all) that all her life she was misunderstood?
That we'd shared a language which for whatever
reasons she herself had never learned? That all
her attempts to draw us in only further served
to hold us apart? That she'd had good reason
to defend as true what we'd perceived as utterly false?
That what she'd said in love or affection we heard
as confusion, anger, fear? Of course, these questions
have no beginning or end, and like posterity
they fuel themselves on a bottomless human vanity:
the illusion that we can "know" someone. And yet
not to go on asking these questions is to follow
that line through time and space that would lead us
to experience her death—conclusively? nostalgically?
consolingly?— as "the final pages of a novel."
And how could she ever forgive us that?

22.

A lead-colored hoarfrost solders the grass
to the staked, transplanted cedars along
the new "park walk" on the hospital grounds,
where a patient empurpled like a fake
carnation nods toward the thousand-
windowed front. It's just past ten, the first
of Sunday's visiting hours, and now,
in broken files, past ghosted, rainbow-
coded signs, the families come forward
from the parking lots . . . which to her
still seem some vast frontier the healthy
into exile cross: dogged, downcast,
hunkered into the cold, drawn in caravan
from the smoke-filled feudal towns beyond.

23.

A dream I started having several weeks ago.
As in the newsreel of some dignitary-or-other
arriving in a foreign country, she's descending alone
the moveable staircase from an airplane cabin,
and as she descends her face grows steadily younger
and more beautiful, like someone "coming into
her own life." But instead of "the pathos of kindled hopes,"
I feel this moment as something that happens
to endanger her, something she is helpless
to defend against, as though the newsreel presaged
an assassin's bomb. This feeling brings with it
a desperate urge to "roll back the film," which succeeds
only in slowing it down to a pace that further
accentuates the dread, as though the newsreel
slowed to capture the instant the bomb goes off.
Each step seems drawn out endlessly, and echoes
so in memory that I almost think I can feel—*in her*—
that earth-bound, raw, quicksilvered weight
a life takes on in that moment it ceases to be a life.

24.

In the last photograph of my sister, she is
sprawling in the shade, or what shade's left,
on the converted toolshed's whitewashed steps.
It appears that she has finished for the day,
an oil color of some tall sea pines, backlit
by twilight off the water behind, her lifelong
childlike forest-fear subdued for the moment
by a filtered-through, delaminating blue
loosening the fretwork of branch and crown.
The oversized sweater she always wore
is stippled with paint, and her face has the slightly
moonstruck look (backlit, as well, by a thin
gilt wash too finely filtered for the camera's lens)
of someone who's stayed up reading late a novel
whose story could be her own.
                              Moments before,
she'd lifted the painting toward the sun, squinting
as she did, imagining—what? we'll never know—
the fading context into which she stared. Then,
unpinning her hair, and leaning back against
the shed, she yawns once and closes her eyes
as if nothing weighed on her thoughts that day,
her shoes kicked off, and an unlit cigarette cupped
in her hand. And at just the instant the shutter
clicks, the shadow of a dog (or a child?) appears
at the far right edge of the picture. To think:
how once she might've been amused by this,

this perspective from which we'd frame her life
(the perspective from which our own deaths hide)
with who she'd been, was, and was tempted to be.

25.

And so it continues, day after day, this endless succession of moments culled haphazard from the staticky dark as though each were an event unto itself, as though each inscribed some legible scratch on the frail wax cylinder that kept alive a voice from the ever-receding past. . . .

My sister at thirty or thirty-one: stripping off table varnish
while her daughters nap on a folded towel beside her.

In the archangel section of the plaster cast gallery, she holds
her breath until the security guard stops looking her way.

Standing beside the photomat, staring at a strip of pictures,
her look of puzzlement slowly gives way to a look of recognition.

In the middle of the night—I was eight or nine at the time—I wake
to find her patting my head, because she has just had a bad dream.

Visiting hours over, she returns down the hall to her hospital room:
head down, shoulders stooped, her hands clasped behind her neck.

(That same morning, when she started to cry, she somehow managed
to distract herself by repeatedly crossing and uncrossing her legs.)

Overjoyed to be finally going home, then, mid-sentence, falling silent
at the thought of it, as though her mouth had been covered by a hand.

A warm spring night. A streetlamp beyond an open window.
Beneath the sill: a girl's hushed voice exhorting itself in whispers.

One morning, she leaves the house before dawn. She doesn't take the car.
By noon she finds herself in the business district of the city—

a taxi is waiting, the driver is holding the door, and she sees that now,
after all these years, she's about to take the great journey of her life.

Four

Abandoned Railway Station

The agent's office like an abbey chancel.
The smell of wood smoke from the baggage stalls.
Large empty walls, and a water stain,
ultramarine, like a fresco of Perseus,
head in hand, fleeing the golden falchion.

The silence of thousands of last goodbyes.
A dried ink pad. Stanchioned ceiling.
And a cognate, terra-cotta dust over
everything, with the on-tiptoe atmosphere
of a *boule-de-neige* before it's shaken.

The Dream of Exile

wafted away to the end of the known world
— Ovid at Tomis

Each weekend, midsummer, alone and with a knapsack
I would set out right around daybreak

from the factory ramp at Merchants Yard,
push off from the shore of my elected home,

and dream above the ugly stream for hours until,
as from a space dilated through my ear-

marked copy of the *Tristia,* one by one the walled
estates would wedge up into that alien air,

their Pompeian glitter raying out like a million
far-flung mercuried coins through the hickory woods,

where I'd drift on my derelict raft, swept along
as if by History past a world perfumed with nard;

then drift some more; then tie up just before
a spill that emptied on the Cumberland

and listen to the water fall, the towrope groaning
with a sound like iron gateposts closing,

and out behind the belt-lashed oar, the light, new-
minted, carried off somewhere, where things

were never what they seemed, and crowds awaited
a glimpse of my black-flagged quinquereme.

Wing Dike at Low Water

I

The Corps of Engineers bulldozed it out
from the limestone bluffs at a point between
a towhead and the shallows, a conscript
calm which pays out water so gradually
its scudding surface seems an image of
the mower's motion, of pale, upended
grain stalks tumbling heavily from the scythe.

II

And yet somewhere below the light bevel
of its watercourse an undercurrent
quarries through acres of sand, gouging out
a barge road in mute, invisible, in-
cessant bursts, which is how we imagine
conscience works, rivering the mind until
the mind's capacities are shaped by it.

III

To make of water a topiary:
declensions in the form of the maple
samara, the slope-backed channel swimmer
shouldering a wave, embodied psalm sound,
hemstitch, a cat's hackle that's been worried

clean. Or Odysseus' arrow punched up
to the feathers in Antínoös' throat.

IV

As though in the air above it spirits
lingered, the drunk at midnight reenacts
(for friends who've given up calling him back)
the myth of the water-walker: braced mid-
river, his arms outreach the multitudes,
all suddenly assumed into the echo-
lalia streaming through him from the dark.

Calypso

I

Although once I blunderingly boasted as much—and no matter
how time after time you've undertaken to recover me from
uncharted hazards on my journey here—I now see that
      I'll never
in my lifetime fathom the way to the trove of that plunder
you've secreted within the pale exposure of your
      outspread limbs.

Take this morning when, as I dressed to leave, you sank back
into the bolstered plush of a feather-printed feather pillow
where, cupping first one breast, and then the other, with
      the thin,
tin, sequined dowel from the Bedouin kohl-bag beside
      your bed,
you marked, so help me, each rounded nipple with a lashing X.

II

"Though at first I suspected the opposite, lately I think your
      pleasure
in me you exaggerate for the sake of what you've left behind.
What you dream of now is home, and her. Don't think I mind,
or mind too much. The truth is, I prefer men pitched
      past hunger
onto the rough feast they inevitably make of a woman's
      forbidden body.

How else to become a goddess? And so, if I let you go,
    you mustn't
mistake it for a kindness. How often these days, when I
    arch back
over you lying in bed, I'm reminded of a marble sculpture
    in Thera,
a headstone where twin dolphins over a flagship leapt, in joy
    or terror
one cannot say, while the awninged ministers yawned and ate."

Orpheus in the Underworld

Still jet-lagged after a fourteen-hour
transatlantic flight held over at Logan
while the weather cleared, his nightlong
fitful tossing in the hotel has at last
subsided into stony sleep, as if into the vast
lowlands he'd descended step by step
through the blurred transparencies
of dread or guilt, while the dark banked
richly below him now seemed in one
broad sweep dispersed by the numbing
counterforce of the Nembutal. It's easy
to imagine how the light of that uplifted calm,
so welcome and while such things last
so absolute, might come to seem a loosening
rainfall just before dusk in the sand-
and-gravel courtyard bordered with grass
of a bed and breakfast near Islandmagee;
or how the mind at rest might slowly form
the sheltered lean-to two people make
as they huddle, smoking, lost in talk
on the stone seat of a planter trough
beside the ever-present murmurings
of the Irish Sea.
                        It's another thing altogether
to imagine how we might see from here
the decision was hers to take or leave,
the decision set out before her now
like a small glass globe nestled into which
the past and future are both disturbed

by a glittering swirl of mixed emotions:
the decision as to whether, at thirty-eight,
she'll leave her widowed father's farm,
her job in a Belfast tinned-meat plant,
and return with him to America. For though
they'd been lovers twenty years ago,
though they'd risen married from a field of hay
in those faraway coppery August days,
more and more those days are edged
with the bright penumbra of an unreal world.
And then there was this other thing. Last night,
as she'd undressed behind the mirrored inlay
of the armoire door, she'd asked him
not to look at her, yet when she'd crossed
the room to bed she couldn't help feel
that the woman he saw (his gaze burned
down her with a flame that numbs) was no longer
the woman he thought he'd known.

        Not seeing
her decision was already at hand, already
foretold in the stars' slow-circling parables,
his thoughts had drifted off somewhere;
and the rainwashed pebbles beneath his feet,
the teary shine they each blinked back
from the flickering gaslamps hung inside,
seemed the sad reminder of a dream
he'd once had as a boy. About a girl
he'd imagined was moving toward him
through all the uncertainties of time and space,

over secret pathways, crossing hidden streams,
and destined like Plato's paradigm
to complete them both in the rounded shell-shape
of a single soul. But having found in those
he'd drawn close to, not a kindred spirit,
not the feeling of two halves joined as one,
but a hemmed in, ripening isolation
at heart, time had proven the cruel chimera
of all such dreams. And was it really so wrong
that he'd wanted to know if someone
who'd loved him years ago
was someone who might now love him again?
What *was* wrong (at least what she thought strange)
was the almost boundless self-concern
he'd dragged behind him all these years,
as if to yearn for love and never to possess it—
like the voiced, unanswered yearning of the sea
she'd listened to nightly all her life—
were not the common fate of humankind.

And so, having settled her mind, having risen
to say goodbye to him for the second and last time
in her life, she turned around to face this man
without any expression of longing or fear,
without any particular expression at all;
and this almost as if by stealth passed out
of the lifting shelter of the dream and into
the waking spirit of the man who was rising
slowly through its counterpanes. And like all

paired sleepers returning to the world
in the pitch and thrall of where they've been,
the man in the airport hotel room felt pulling away,
withdrawing from him, like a coin down-trailing
through the reaches of a well, the dimming
features of her upturned face. But it wasn't until
he'd boarded the final leg of his flight,
until he'd finished his second gin-and-bitters
and sagged back against the windowframe,
that he felt it release its hold on him:
the heavy and strangely lingering effect,
or aftereffect, of the Nembutal. A drug
whereby the mind slides easily out of itself,
and views its failings as if from the air.

Belfast Arioso

She is standing in the kitchen preparing a roast.
He stands beside her uncorking the wine.
It's early evening; a live opera is on
the BBC. She is wearing a pair of earrings

he just bought at the co-op the day before:
red-leaded, rectangular glass the sun
through the skylight does not inflame,
however brightly he'd imagined it would.

He pours a small glass for each of them,
she raises hers, and though I can't tell what
they are saying, it appears that she is singing
to him, and he is answering back in song.

Back and forth they sing to each other, each
in turn determined to fill the silence settling
around them like a story their song can't quite
dispel. But whose story is it, after all?

Theirs? Ours? History's own? as history claims.
(In the opera, it usually belongs to the one
who's killed, a violence we perceive
as beauty.) She sets the timer on the oven clock.

He clears his throat with a second glass.
And now they're dancing, arm in arm,
dancing across the bare, swept flagstones
of the kitchen floor. It seems so familiar

who'd think to ask if they'll still be here
at the story's end? Or, if not, if they'll
be summoned when the world applauds
the art of catastrophe their singing formed.

Thresholds

from the Irish of Cathal Ó Searcaigh

The Other World

Your downward dreamlife refuses to build
either a sanctuary or a military barracks.

For hours tonight I've trespassed freely
in that far-flung space behind your eyes,

much more at home in the blueness there
than in the Virgin's tendered muslin sash.

On the other side of words, surely
there must be another word for this.

Sun Rush

From *Mín na Craoibhe* to *Gort a' Choirce,*
the glen, sun-scoured since morning,
gleams in a sudden rinse of gold.

And now the labored breathers come,
Sunday's rayed conquistadores,
laying claim to their fair share of sun.

Of Kinship and the Spoken Word

"We are all of us brothers"
said the monk to my father
as he stood at our door
and slowly unfolded a fat
pink palm. But when once,
in jest, I unthinkingly crossed
the narrowing threshold
of his piety—"like Cain
and Abel, I suppose?"—
the well-worn knife blade
of his sidelong glance
pricked out a blood drop
on my cheek and heart.

The Poet at Three

"That's pig slop! Dirt clabber, you little shit,"
my father's foulmouthed outbursts stormed,
while I pitched happily in the mud gully
running beside the road. "Out with you
from that clabber before you catch your death!"

But I just kept on wallowing, messing about,
delighted to raise my song to muck:
"Clabber! Clabber! It's my own clabber!"
Tyro that I was, the word meant little

until I felt the skin-deep squelch of wellies,
and through the sop of my drenched clothes
the sudden chill knowledge of water.

Ah! clabber of destiny, soaked to bone.

Ghost Sonnet

The offshore rains had come early to the headlands, the pools
of standing water quickly filling into streams, the wind
green-scented with the high grass thickening the margins
of the road. For a day and a half I'd slogged up through it
circling the bog beneath Queen Maeve's cairn. But just toward
dusk of that second day, as when a jostled memory's loosed
from some dark mooring in the head, the wet mist lifted, the
last
thin wisps drawn off like topsails from the ditchbacks and ferns.
And then the wind whistled, in Yeats's phrase, history-
haunted round the Mareotic Lake, and the sun-scrubbed win-
dows
of the drying sheds gave back that last clear-vowelled light,
their canted roofs afloat in the hills like those storied stone
boats
idling on the tide—or like the scatter of his unsettling swans,
which I now know can neither be found nor forgotten.

A Tulip in Winter

Your out-of-season hospital tulip still
brightens above its parti-colored foil.

Lacquered in lamplight, its fleshy leafage
could, conceivably, survive this way

a hundred days. A hundred days (imagine
that) to paint out the wallpaper harlequins,

uncane your cane-back rocking chair,
to reclaim your green connection to a place

where flowers such as these are grown
to leave the living less impossibly alone.

Notes

"The Story": *Hasidic Tales of the Holocaust,* Yaffa Eliach (Oxford University Press, 1982).

PART TWO

"The Whelk": "*poppies ran like torchmen . . .*" I am grateful to John Hollander's *American Poetry: The Nineteenth Century* (The Library of America, 1993), which led me back to the poetry of Helen Hunt Jackson. Born in Amherst, Massachusetts, Jackson was an early and lifelong friend of Emily Dickinson. In her mid-forties, after losing two sons to illness, and her husband to an accident while testing a submarine device, she traveled to and eventually settled in Colorado Springs. The line is from her poem "Poppies on the Wheat," which recalls her native coast and the torchmen who'd run to mark the shoreline for passing ships. Upon learning of her death, Emily Dickinson wrote, "Helen of Troy will die, but Helen of Colorado, never."

"Tahoe Nocturne": "*Do you have the poems . . .*" and "*these words that no one . . .*" from Han-shan's *Cold Mountain,* translated by Burton Watson (Shambhala, 1992).

PART FOUR

"Thresholds": Cathal Ó Searcaigh, poet and playwright, lives on a small hill farm at the foot of Mount Errigal in County Donegal. My thanks to him for his patient and much-needed guidance with these translations, which derive from four unlinked poems in *Homecoming/An bealach 'na bhaile* (Cló Iar-Chonnachta, 1993).